The Anxious Dragon

by **Emma Hanna**
Illustrations **Connie Duncan**

If I asked you to close your eyes
And picture a dragon in your mind,
I wonder what you would see
Or what your imagination might find.

For me he would be scaly green
And from his mouth come flames.
He'd be brave and strong and ruthless,
Not the type for fun and games!

But the dragon in our story
Is not like that at all.
He looks a bit like all the others
But inside he feels so small.

When you look at his face
And his scales so tough and green,
You'd think he was quite scary
And really rather mean.

No, the dragon I want to talk about
Is a dear old friend of mine
And he's been having a bit of trouble
At this particular time.

You see the problem with this dragon
Is that his anxiety gets him down.
Instead of feeling tough and strong
He often wears a frown.

When it's time for school
Or to go to the park with friends,
My dragon chum gets butterflies –
A feeling that never seems to end.

He described them once
Like giant moths flying in his tummy.
They make him cry and feel so sad
He has to tell his mummy.

But he doesn't think she understands
How awful it makes him feel.
He wishes he could show her
How his feelings are so real.

He worries all the time
About what other people see.
He worries if he's done something wrong
And "What must they think of me?"

Having somewhere new to go
Sends his anxiety off the scale.
He tries to make excuses
But then his friends will only wail.

He plays around like normal,
But inside his little head
There are tons and tons of worries
That make him just want to go to bed.

But when he goes to bed
He finds it hard to sleep
Because the thoughts inside his brain
Just make him want to weep.

He tried a few times to talk
To some of the teachers at school,
But they were always very busy
And he felt like such a fool.

One day he cancelled with his friends
And wouldn't meet them at the park,
But they got cross with him and asked,
"Why are you keeping us in the dark?

"We can see there's something wrong
And we'd love it if you'd tell.
Is there something we have done
Or don't you feel too well?"

The dragon sighed and blew a flame –
He was going to have to talk.
His friends were going to listen
And then away they'd probably walk.

"I always feel really nervous.
I'm anxious all day long.
I worry if I've done things right
Or what I've said is wrong.

"These big black moths inside me
Make me feel quite sick.
It sounds so silly when I say this –
I'm not a friend you'd pick.

"I'd love to be more like you guys
And be confident and cool,
But I can't get these worries from my head –
I feel even worse at school.

"I hate it when the teacher says
We have to read aloud.
I get all flustered and all sweaty –
I feel the opposite of proud.

"My heart beats really quickly
And there'll be sweat upon my scales
My tongue gets tied up inside my mouth
And my green skin goes quite pale.

"I understand if you would like
Our friendship to come to an end.
I've tried everything to help myself –
I'm just a useless friend."

The dragon's friends looked worried,
Concern was in their eyes.
They didn't really know what to say
But there was no way it was goodbye!

"We'd like to help you with your nerves.
Your anxiety we can't mend,
But we can surely stick with you –
Please remember, we're your friends."

They looked on the internet
For ideas to help their dragon chum.
They found there were lots of ways
To help him feel less glum.

One found out that breathing deeply
Would help to calm him down.
He just had to take care with blowing flames
Or his neighbours would surely frown!

"Breathe in through your nose," they said,
"And inside your head count to three,
Then breathe out very slowly,
Count to six, then wait and see.

"If you do this when you're anxious
Or feeling very uptight,
You might find that it helps you.
Let us know if we are right.

"Different things help different dragons
So it's a case of testing options out.
You could try this thing called tapping
It will help without a doubt.

"You tap your head and chest
And other pressure points,
Then you acknowledge how you're feeling —
I promise it won't disappoint."

"It works for my mum," one dragon said.
"She taps at times of doubt,
And the more times that she does it
The more it helps her out."

The dragon looked at all his friends
And realised how lucky he was.
They were each so happy to help him
And it made him stop and pause.

He'd hidden his secret feelings
Out of worry and of shame,
But his anxiety didn't scare them off –
They loved him just the same.

Once he even tried yoga
But he said, "Never again!"
He caught his claw, then burnt the mat
And ended up in quite a lot of pain!

He always tries to conquer it
And is working on different techniques.
He wishes there was an easy way
Or a magic spell that he could speak!

But unfortunately there isn't —
That's the thing he has to accept,
But opening up to his friends
Is something he'll never regret.

When he gets that feeling in his tummy
Of those great big butterflies,
He tells his friends they're back again —
Sometimes he even cries.

Of course not everyone got it –
That would take some time.
He didn't understand anxiety himself
But at least he knew it wasn't a crime.

So that is where we leave our friend
And I'm happy to declare
That although his anxiety hasn't gone
His friends are all still there.

Now at least he's got more control
And ways that improve how he feels.
Some day he's sure it will disappear
And our dragon friend might be healed!